To Kerry on your 6th Birthday

Lots of Love from

Mandy, Roy, & Lisa

XX

X

NOW YOU CAN READ MORE STORIES

ADAPTED BY LUCY KINCAID
ILLUSTRATED BY
ERIC ROWE · ERIC KINCAID · PAMELA STOREY
GILLIAN EMBLETON · GEORGINA HARGREAVES

BRIMAX BOOKS · CAMBRIDGE · ENGLAND

The stories and illustrations
in this Omnibus have been
published as separate volumes
by Brimax Books

Published by Brimax Books,
Cambridge, England 1981
Third Printing 1983
ISBN 0 86112 029 9
Printed in Hong Kong

CONTENTS

Snow White
and the Seven Dwarfs

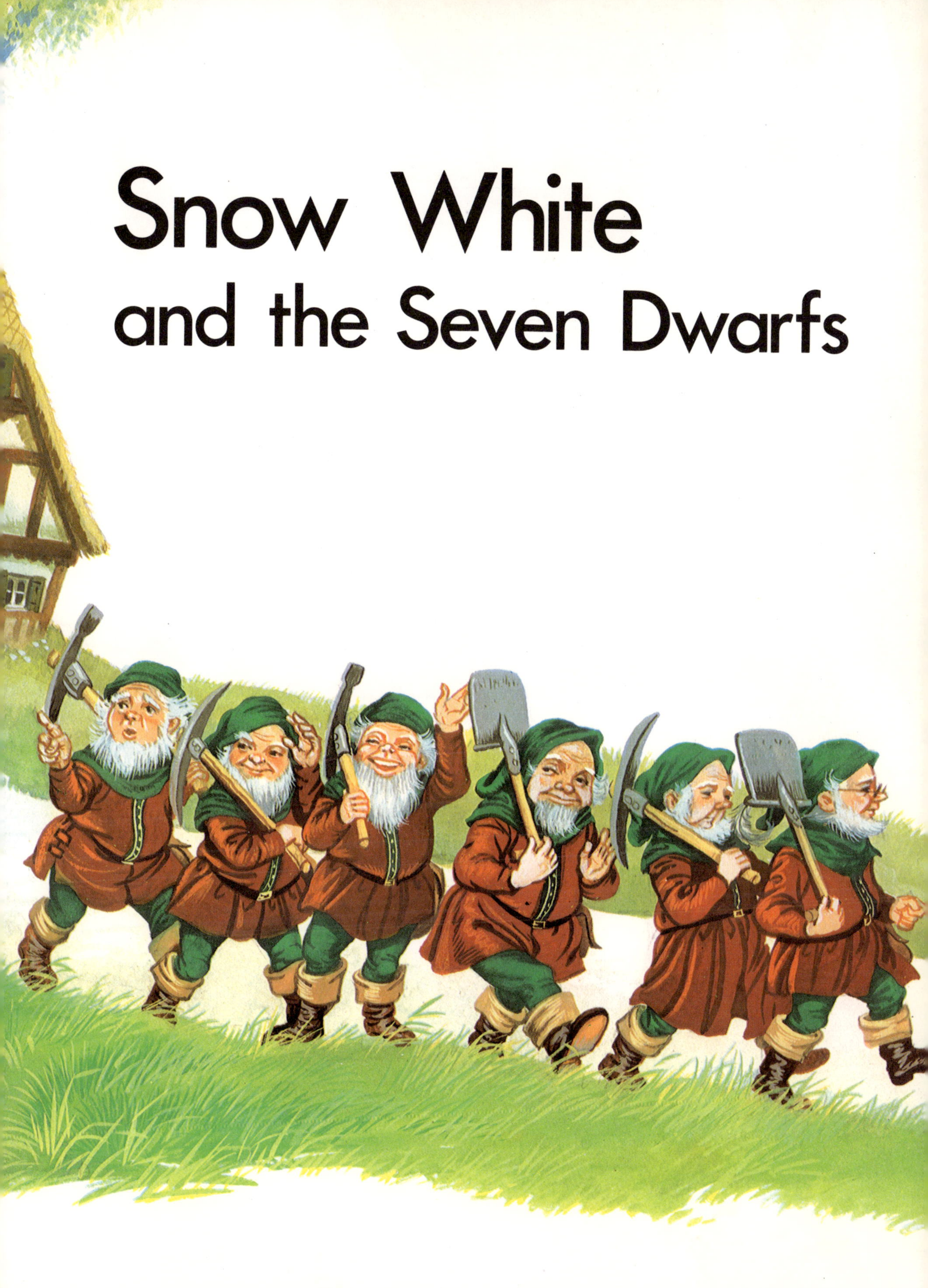

Once there was a wicked Queen who had a magic mirror. Every day she would say,
"Mirror, mirror on the wall,
Who is the fairest of them all?"
Every day the mirror would reply,
"You, oh Queen,
Are the fairest in all the land."

One day, the Queen asked,
"Mirror, mirror on the wall,
Who is the fairest of them all?"
And the mirror replied,
"You, oh Queen, are very fair,
But Snow White is the fairest in all the land."

Instead of her own face looking from the mirror the Queen saw the face of her step-daughter. She was VERY angry.

She sent for her huntsman. “Take Snow White into the forest and kill her,” she said.

The huntsman loved Snow White. “I cannot kill you,” he said. “But I cannot take you home either. You must stay here, in the forest.”

The huntsman returned to the palace alone. He told the Queen he had killed Snow White.

Snow White wandered through the dark forest. She did not know where to go, or what to do. Presently she came to a little house. "Perhaps the people who live here will help me," she said. She knocked at the door. There was no reply, so she peeped inside.

What an untidy house it was. Every thing in it was smaller than usual. And there seemed to be seven of EVERYTHING. Seven chairs. Seven beds. Seven spoons. Seven plates. Seven mugs. Seven of EVERYTHING . . . except tables. There was just one table.

"Perhaps children who have lost their mother live here," said Snow White. "I will tidy the house for them."

She swept, and dusted and cleaned and polished. She had plenty of helpers.

There was a diamond mine on the far side of the forest. It was worked by seven dwarfs. The very same dwarfs who lived in the house Snow White had found. They were on their way home. What would happen to Snow White now?

"Who . . . who are you?" asked Snow White. "This is our house," said the seven dwarfs all together. "We work in the diamond mine on the far side of the forest. Do not be afraid, we will not hurt you. Just tell us what are YOU doing in OUR house?"

Snow White told the dwarfs what had happened.

"You can stay here with us. We will look after you." said the dwarfs.

"And I will look after you," said Snow White. "I will cook and sew and clean for you."

And she did. And they were all very happy.

But the dwarfs were afraid the wicked Queen would come looking for Snow White one day. "Do not answer the door to anyone," they said, whenever they went to the mine.

They were right to be worried.

"Mirror, mirror on the wall,
Who is the fairest of them all?"
asked the Queen.
"You, oh Queen, are very fair,
But Snow White, who lives in the forest with the little men, is the fairest in all the land."
The Queen was VERY ANGRY INDEED. "I will kill Snow White myself!" she said.

The Queen disguised herself as a pedlar. She filled a basket with apples then went into the forest. She waited until the dwarfs had gone to the mine, then she knocked at the door of the little house.

"I have nothing to fear from a pedlar," said Snow White. And though the dwarfs had warned her not to open the door, she did.

"Good day child," said the Queen. "Would you like one of my apples?" "Yes please . . ." said Snow White.

The Queen gave Snow White the reddest apple in the basket. It was a special apple. A VERY special apple. The Queen had put a spell on it.

"Take a bite . . ." said the Queen. Snow White took just one bite from the apple and fell to the floor. "Ha! Ha!" laughed the Queen, and she threw off her disguise. "Snow White is dead. Now I am the fairest in all the land!"

When the dwarfs came home they found Snow White lying on the floor. They found the apple, with one bite taken from it, lying beside her. "The wicked Queen has been here," they said sadly. "Snow White is dead!"

The dwarfs built a special bed for Snow White in the forest. The birds and the animals kept watch around her.

One day a prince came riding by and saw her lying there.
"Please let me take her home," he said.

As the Prince lifted Snow White onto his horse she opened her eyes. The piece of magic apple had fallen from her throat. The spell cast by the wicked Queen was broken. "Snow White is alive!" shouted the dwarfs. "Hoorah! Hoorah!"

Once more, the Queen asked the magic mirror who was the fairest of them all.

The mirror replied,

"You, oh Queen, are very fair,
But Snow White, the Prince's bride,
is the fairest in all the land."

The Queen was so angry, she flew into a rage and died herself. And so Snow White was safe at last.

All these appear in the pages of the story. Can you find them?

Queen

mirror

Snow White

huntsman

forest

dwarfs

apple

Prince

Use the pictures to tell the story in your own words, and then draw your own pictures.

Rumpelstiltskin

Once there was a miller who had a beautiful daughter. He was always boasting about her. Sometimes he said things that were not true.

One day he said, "My daughter is so clever she can spin straw into gold."

The King heard about the miller's daughter and sent for her.
"You shall spin straw into gold for ME!" he said.
The miller's daughter wanted to say that was impossible, but she had never seen a king before and she was afraid to speak.

The King took her to a room where there was a spinning wheel and a pile of straw.

"If you value your life," he said sternly, "You will spin all that straw into gold by morning."

And then, he left the room and locked the door behind him.

The miller's daughter began to cry. She did not know WHAT to do. Then, through her tears, she saw a tiny man with a long white beard, standing beside the spinning wheel.

"What will you give me if I spin the straw into gold for you?" he asked.

"I will give you my necklace," she said, quickly drying her tears.

The next morning, when the King unlocked the door, the straw was gone. In its place was a heap of gold. The miller's daughter was sorting the golden coins into piles.

That night the King led her back to the same room. This time the straw stretched from wall to wall and reached as high as the windowsill.

"If you value your life," said the King sternly, "Spin all THAT into gold by morning."

As soon as the door was locked the little man appeared. "What will you give me if I help you this time?" he asked. "My ring," replied the miller's daughter, taking the ring from her finger.

When the King saw the huge pile of gold next morning he was very pleased. He led the miller's daughter straight to a room where the straw was piled so high it touched the ceiling.

"Spin all THAT into gold and you shall be my Queen," he said.

As soon as the door was locked the little man appeared beside the spinning wheel.
"I have nothing left to give you," said the miller's daughter sadly.
"Give me the first child born to you when you are Queen," said the little man.
The miller's daughter wanted to be Queen so she agreed. The little man began to spin.

A few days later the miller's daughter married the King, and became Queen. What a lot of boasting her father did THAT day!

A whole year went by and the new Queen forgot about the little man who had come to help her. Then, one day, there was great excitement at the palace. A baby had been born.

The excitement quickly changed to weeping and wailing when the little man appeared.

"I will give you all the treasure in the treasure house, if only you will let me keep my baby," wept the Queen.

"You made a promise. You must keep it," said the little man.

But the Queen made so much fuss and held the baby so tightly that at last he said to the Queen, "You may keep the child if you can tell me my name within the next three days."

The Queen lay awake, thinking, all night. "Is your name Grizzlebeard?" she asked, next morning.

"No!"

"Is it Firkin?"

"It is not!"

"Is it Bodkin?"

"No!"

On the second day, after another sleepless night, the Queen asked, "Is your name Shortlegs?"

"No!"

"Is it Longears?"

"No!"

"Is it Pipkin?"

"No!"

The Queen just HAD to get the name right. She sent her servants far and wide across the land in search of names that were strange or unusual. One of the grooms was riding through a wood when he heard someone singing.
He stopped his horse and got off.

He crept closer and saw a little man dancing round a fire of twigs and leaves. He was singing to himself,

"Today I bake, tomorrow brew.
What a clever thing I do.
Soon a baby I will claim.
Rumpelstiltskin is my name."

The servant galloped back to the palace as fast as he could. He told the Queen all that he had seen and heard.

The next day, when the little man appeared at the palace, the Queen asked, “Is your name Harry?”

“No!”

“Is it Timothy?”

“No!”

“Could it be . . . Rumpelstiltskin?”

"A witch must have told you THAT!" shouted the little man in a rage. He was so angry he stamped his foot far too hard and it went right through the floor. He had to pull it out with his hands.

But he had made a promise, and he kept to it. The baby was safe.

All these appear in the pages of the story. Can you find them.

Use the pictures to tell the story in your own words, and then draw your own pictures.

Cinderella

Cinderella lived in a big house. She was ALWAYS busy. Her two step-sisters made sure of that.

"Cinderella! Sweep the floor!"

"Cinderella! Wash the dishes!"

"Make the beds!"

"Clean the windows!"

Cinderella's work was NEVER done.

Cinderella's step-sisters spent half the day telling her what to do. They spent the other half trying to look pretty.

"Cinderella! Brush my hair!"

"Cinderella! Tie my bow!"

"Powder my nose!"

"Fasten my buttons!"

One day a letter arrived at the house. "There is to be a ball at the palace! We are invited!" shouted the step-sisters. "Am I invited?" asked Cinderella. "Even if you are, you cannot go," said her step-sisters. "You will be too busy getting US ready!"

The day of the ball came. The step-sisters kept Cinderella VERY busy indeed. There was SO much to do. Poor Cinderella did not know what to do first.

At last, the step-sisters had gone, and the house was quiet. Cinderella sat by the fire and began to cry.

"If only I could have gone to the ball," she wept.

"You shall go to the ball!" said a voice behind her.

Cinderella jumped up in alarm. She thought she was alone in the house.

"Who . . . who are you?" she gasped.

"I am your Fairy Godmother," said the stranger. "I have come to get YOU ready for the ball."

"Bring me a pumpkin!" said the Fairy Godmother. She turned the pumpkin into a coach.

"Bring me four white mice!" said the Fairy Godmother. She turned the mice into four white horses.

"Bring me three lizards!" said the Fairy Godmother. They became a coach-driver, and two footmen.

“I cannot go to the ball dressed in rags,” said Cinderella sadly.

The Fairy Godmother waved her magic wand once more. Cinderella's rags turned into a beautiful ball gown. Her bare feet were covered with dainty glass slippers.
"Now YOU are ready for the ball," said the Fairy Godmother.

"But first, a warning. You must leave before the clock strikes twelve. At twelve everything will change back to the way it was before."

"I will remember," said Cinderella. "Thank you, dear Fairy Godmother."

Cinderella danced all night with the Prince. Her step-sisters saw her, but they did not recognise her. They thought she was a visiting princess.

Cinderella was so happy she forgot all about the Fairy Godmother's warning. She did not remember until the palace clock began to strike the chimes of midnight. One . . . two . . . three . . . "I must go!" she cried, and ran from the palace.

"Stop! Stop!"
cried the Prince.
Cinderella did not
hear him.
As she ran down
the palace steps
she lost one of
her glass slippers.

ten . . . eleven . . .
TWELVE!!!!!
The beautiful gown
turned into rags.
The coach turned
into a pumpkin.
The mice and
lizards ran away.

The Prince found her glass slipper lying on the palace steps. He called a footman. "Take this slipper and find its owner. I will marry the girl it fits."

The footman travelled all over the kingdom with the slipper. It fitted no one. At last he came to the house where Cinderella lived. "Let me try it!" said one of her step-sisters. She snatched the slipper from the footman.

“Look!” she cried. “A perfect fit!”

“No it isn’t!” shouted the other step-sister. “Your heel is hanging out! Give it to me!” And SHE snatched the glass slipper.

It didn't fit her either. Though she tried to pretend that it did. "Is there anyone else in the house who should try the slipper?" asked the footman.

"NO!" said both step-sisters together.
"Yes there is," said their father. "Cinderella hasn't tried it yet."
"The Prince would never marry HER!" laughed the step-sisters.

"The Prince said EVERYONE must try the slipper," said the footman. It fitted Cinderella perfectly. Her step-sisters were so surprised, they fainted.

The Prince DID marry Cinderella. The step-sisters were at the wedding. They still looked surprised.

All these appear in the pages of the story. Can you find them?

Use the pictures to tell the story in your own words, and then draw your own pictures.

Puss in Boots

Once there was a miller who had three sons. When he died he left his eldest son the mill. He left his second eldest son the donkey. He had nothing to leave John, his youngest son, except the cat.

John's brothers laughed. "You will never make a fortune with a cat," they said.

“Master” said the cat when John and he were alone. “Buy me a pair of boots and I WILL make you a fortune.” It was plain to see the cat was no ordinary cat.

John did as the cat asked. He bought him a pair of boots. The cat put them on.

"Now give me a sack and I will go hunting," said Puss in Boots, as he was to be known from then on.

Puss in Boots went into the forest. He caught a rabbit. Instead of taking it home to John he took it to the King's palace. "I have a present for the King," he said.

"I am Puss in Boots," he said to the King. "I have brought you a present from my master, the Marquis of Carrabas."

"Thank you very much," said the King. Kings are like everyone else. They like getting presents.

Puss in Boots went hunting every day. Everything he caught he took to the King. Every day he said, "This is a present from my master the Marquis of Carrabas."

One day, the King said, "I would like to meet your master. I will call my coach. You can take me to see him."

"I cannot ride with you," said Puss in Boots. "I have some business to attend to. I will meet you at my master's castle."

"Very well!" said the King.

The Princess said she would ride with the King. They got into the coach and set off.

On the way they passed some men working in the fields. "Who owns this land?" called the King. "The Marquis of Carrabas!" answered the men. Puss in Boots had already passed that way. HE had told the men what to say if the King spoke to them.

There were men cutting wood in the forest. "Who owns THIS land?" called the King.

"The Marquis of Carrabas!" replied the wood cutters. Puss in Boots had told THEM what to say too.

"The Marquis of Carrabas must be a very rich man," said the King.

When Puss in Boots got home he called to John. "Quick master! Go to the river and bathe."

"Why?" asked John.

"Just do as I say!" said Puss in Boots.

John was puzzled but he did as he was told. He was even more puzzled when Puss ran off with his clothes and hid them under a bush.

"Help! Help!" called Puss in Boots when he saw the King's coach coming. "Help! Help! My master, the Marquis of Carrabas, is drowning!"

"Someone has stolen my master's clothes," said Puss, when John was rescued.

The King lent John his cloak and invited him to ride in the royal coach.

"The Marquis of Carrabas is very handsome," thought the Princess.

"My master's castle is just over the next hill," said Puss in Boots. "I will run on ahead and prepare for your arrival."

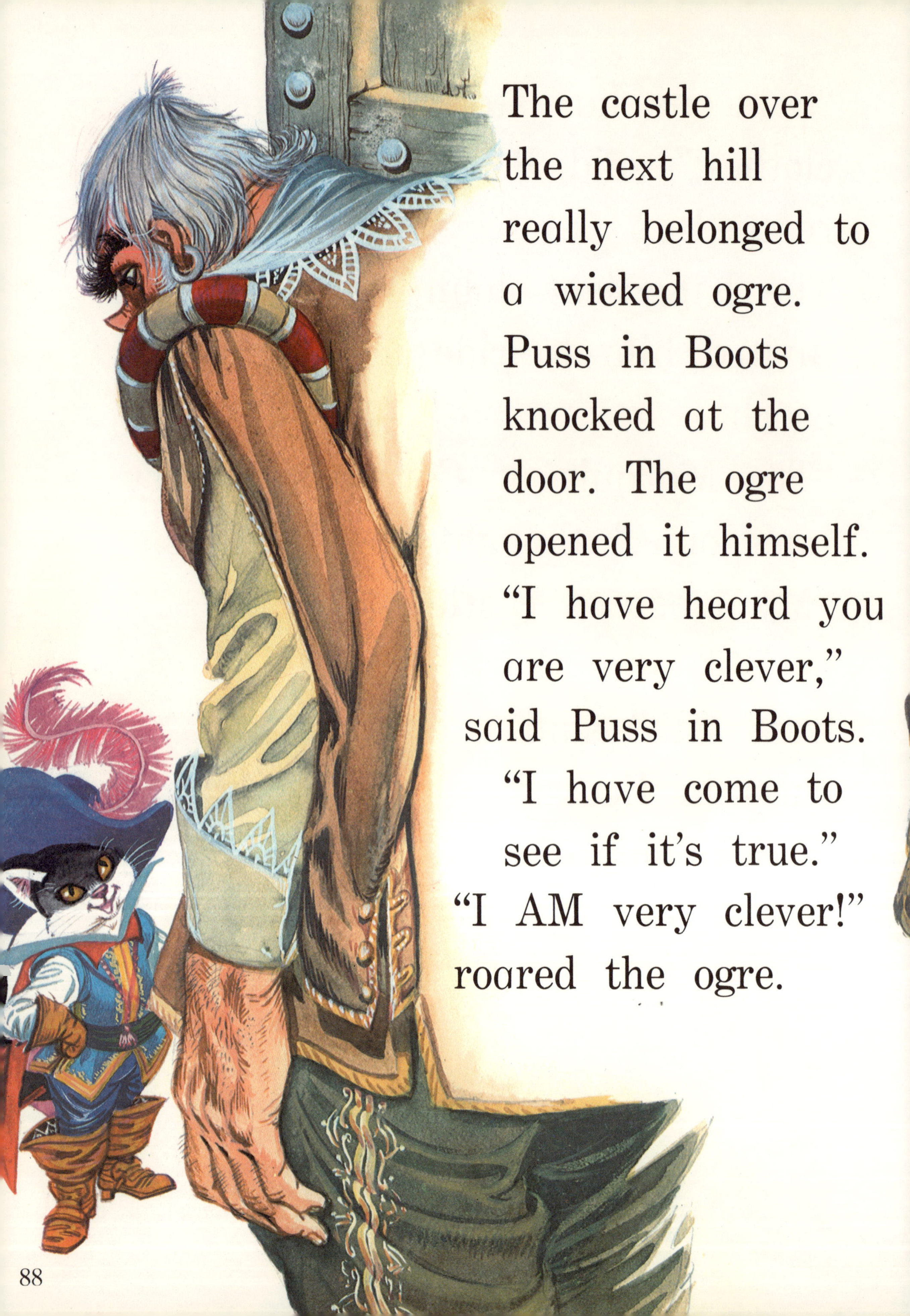

The castle over
the next hill
really belonged to
a wicked ogre.
Puss in Boots
knocked at the
door. The ogre
opened it himself.
"I have heard you
are very clever,"
said Puss in Boots.
"I have come to
see if it's true."
"I AM very clever!"
roared the ogre.

"I can change myself into ANYTHING I please." The ogre snapped his fingers and changed himself into a lion. He growled at Puss in Boots. Puss pretended not to be afraid.

"It's EASY to change into something big," said Puss in Boots. "I don't suppose you can change yourself into something as small as . . . as small as a mouse!"

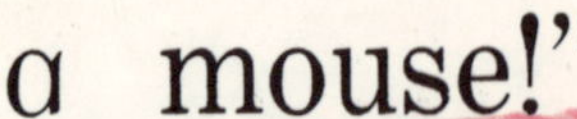

"OH, YES I CAN!" roared the ogre. AND HE DID. But before he could change back again Puss in Boots gobbled him up. And that was the end of the ogre.

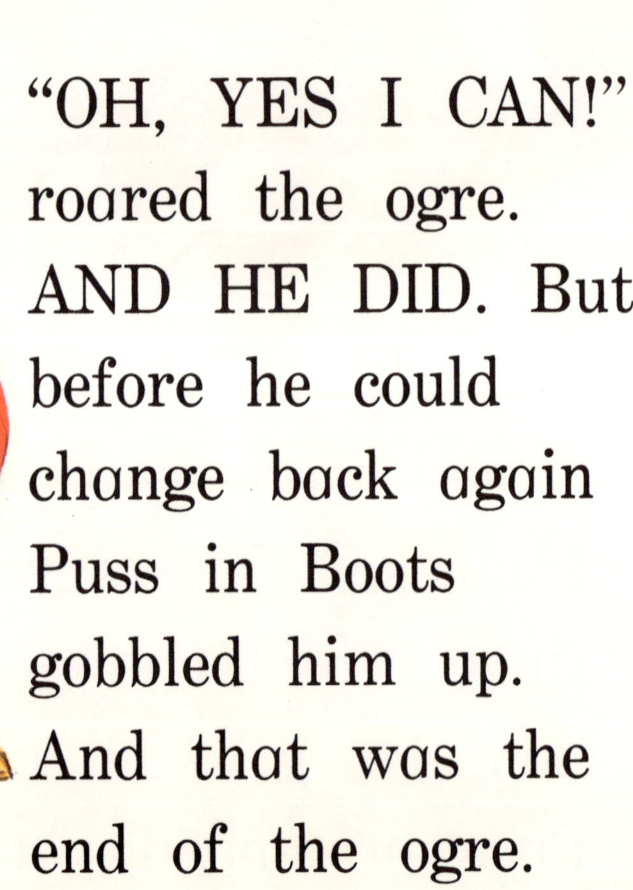

"You have a new master now," said Puss in Boots to the people who lived in the castle. "He is the Marquis of Carrabas. The King is bringing him here now. We must prepare a feast."

"Hooray for the King!" they shouted. "Hooray for the Marquis!"

"HOORAY FOR PUSS IN BOOTS!"

When the King's coach arrived Puss in Boots was waiting at the castle door.

"Welcome! Welcome to the castle of the Marquis of Carrabas," he said.

"Who IS this Marquis of Carrabas?" whispered John.

"YOU are!" said Puss in Boots.

"Am I?" said John. He was very surprised.

John married the Princess, and they lived in the castle. Many years later, they moved into the palace and John became King. Puss in Boots HAD made John's fortune for him, just as he said he would.

All these appear in the pages of the story. Can you find them?

Use the pictures to tell the story in your own words, and then draw your own pictures.

The Ugly Duckling

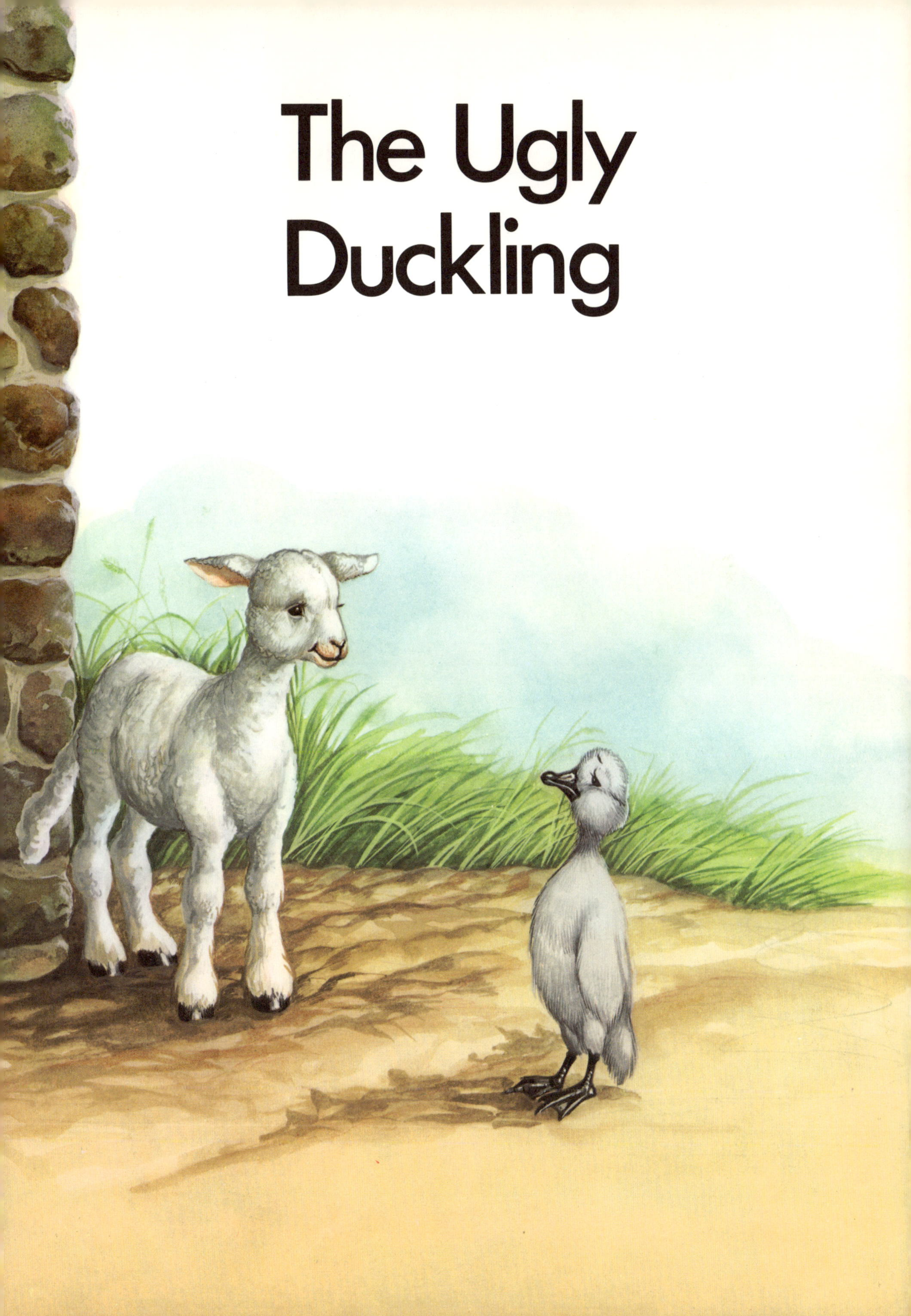

Mother Duck had five broken egg shells, and five new ducklings. She had one egg which did not have a crack in it.

"I wonder when that egg will hatch," said Mother Duck.

Everyone who lived in the farmyard came to look at the egg.

"That is too big to be a duck's egg," said a chicken.

"That will hatch into a turkey, you mark my words," said a goose.

"How will I know if it is a turkey?" asked Mother Duck.

"It will not swim," said the goose.

At last the egg hatched. The bird which stepped from the broken shell did not look like his brothers and sisters at all. But he was not a turkey for he went straight to the pond and began to swim.

"What an ugly little duckling you are," laughed the chickens.

"What an ugly little duckling you are," laughed the geese.
"What an ugly little duckling you are," laughed the other ducks.

The little duckling was so unhappy. He had no friends. EVERYONE laughed at him, even his mother. He decided to run away. "Nobody will miss me," he said. And nobody did.

He made his home on the marshes. One day he saw some wild ducks swimming in a pool. "Will you be my friends?" he asked.

"What an ugly little duckling you are," laughed the wild ducks. "We do not want you in our pool." They chased him away.

One day the little duckling saw some swans flying across the sky. "I wish I were a swan," he said. "Swans are beautiful. Nobody laughs at them." He felt sadder than ever as he watched them fly away.

Winter came. The days were cold. The nights were even colder. Food was very hard to find.

Now the little duckling was not only lonely, he was cold and hungry too.

One cold night the lake froze. When morning came the duckling's feet were stuck firmly in the ice. He could not move.

"Now I will die," he said.

A farmer was taking his dog for a walk. He saw the duckling stuck in the ice.

"We must get you out of there," he said.

The farmer broke the ice with a stick. The little duckling was free again.

"Go and find your friends," said the farmer.
"I wish I had a friend to find," said the little duckling sadly.

The winter was very long but it did not last for ever. Spring came. The days grew warmer. There was plenty to eat. The wild ducks and the wild geese came back to the lake. They had all been away for the winter.

They dabbled and they splashed about in the water and all tried to talk at once.
They had so many things to tell one another. But nobody spoke to the little duckling.
"I wish they would talk to me," he said.

The little duckling watched the wild ducks stretch their wings. He stretched his own wings. He flapped them. And then he flew, for the very first time. Up, up and up, he went, up into the clear blue sky.

He should have been happy, but he did not feel happy. He looked down at the ground far below him. He could see the swans swimming in a pond in a beautiful garden. He would ask them to help him.

He flew down to the pond and settled on the water. He called to the swans. “Please come and kill me. I am so ugly, and I am so lonely I do not want to live.”

"Ugly? You?" said the swans looking surprised. "Have you looked at yourself in the pond?"

The little duckling looked down into the water. Looking back at him was a swan.

"Is . . . is that me?" he asked.
"Of course it is," said the swans.
"But I am beautiful," he said.
"Of course you are," said the swans.
"You are a swan. All swans are beautiful."

Three children came running to the pond.

"Look!" they cried. "A new swan. Please stay in our pond. We will come and see you every day."

The little duckling had changed into a beautiful swan during the long cold winter. He would never be lonely again.

All these appear in the pages of the story. Can you find them?

Mother Duck

chicken

goose

duckling

Use the pictures to tell the story in your own words, and then draw your own pictures.

Sleeping Beauty

A Princess had been born at the palace.
"We must make sure she has all a Princess should have," said the King. "We must invite the fairies to her christening."

"How many fairies live in our Kingdom?" asked the Queen. "Seven," said the King. "We must invite them all."

So the King sent invitations to each one. The King had seven golden caskets made as gifts for the seven fairies.

The day of the christening came. All the guests were sitting in the great palace hall. Suddenly the door flew open. Standing in the doorway was a very angry fairy.

"That is the fairy who lives at the bottom of the well," whispered the King. "I thought she had moved away. We did not send her an invitation."

"No invitation! No golden casket!" shouted the fairy. "How dare you treat a fairy like this! What have you to say for yourself?"

"Come and sit beside me," said the King, trying to keep calm. He did not know what to say. "I am so glad you could come."

When the party was over, the fairies stood round the cradle. They had gifts for the baby Princess.

It came to the seventh fairy's turn to give the Princess a gift.

"Where is the seventh fairy?" asked the King.

"Where is the seventh fairy?" asked the Queen.

Nobody knew where she was.

"We cannot wait for her," said the fairy who had been forgotten. "I want to give my gift to the Princess."

Everyone held his breath. Was she still angry?

"My gift shall be this," said the fairy with a sly smile. "The Princess shall prick her finger on a spindle and DIE!"

The King and Queen wept. Nobody knew what to do. It was then that the seventh fairy came back.

"Do not weep," she said. "I too have a gift for the Princess. She will prick her finger it is true, but she will not die. She will sleep for one hundred years instead."

Everyone went home. The Queen dried her tears. The Princess slept in her cradle.

The King ordered that all the spindles in the kingdom be destroyed. "If there are no spindles, the Princess cannot prick her finger on one," he said.

Sixteen years passed. One day the Princess went for a walk. She came to a tumbledown cottage. She pushed open the door and peeped inside. There was an old woman sitting by the window. She had a spindle in her hand. She was spinning thread. "Come along in," called the old woman.

"What are you doing?" asked the Princess.

"I am spinning," said the old woman.

The Princess watched the spindle twirl.

"Would you like to twirl the spindle?" asked the old woman.

“Yes please,” said the Princess. She sat by the window and took the spindle from the old woman. “Just a little faster,” said the old woman. “Like this?” said the Princess. “Faster . . . faster . . .” said the old woman.

“Oh!” cried the Princess. “I have pricked my finger.” She fell to the floor in a deep sleep. She slept so soundly nobody could wake her.

The seventh fairy heard what had happened to the poor Princess who was taken back to the palace and laid on her bed. The seventh fairy cast a spell that made everyone else in the palace sleep as soundly as the Princess.

"Now the Princess will not be alone when she wakes," said the fairy.

A thick, thorny hedge grew up round the palace and hid it. The years passed by. Strange stories were told about what lay behind the hedge. Many people tried to cut a way through it, but nobody could.

One hundred years after the Princess had fallen asleep along came a Prince. The hedge seemed to melt at the touch of his sword. He could not believe what he saw. All over the palace there were people who had fallen asleep in the middle of what they had been doing.

There were cooks in the middle of cooking, maids in the middle of sweeping and pageboys in the middle of fighting. There were footmen in the middle of carrying messages, lords in the middle of talking and ladies in the middle of dressing. The Prince had to laugh.

When the Prince saw the sleeping Princess he kissed her. She opened her eyes and smiled at him. As she woke the palace clocks started ticking.

Then everyone else in the palace woke too and carried on with what they had been doing one hundred years before. They all lived happily ever after.

All these appear in the pages of the story. Can you find them?

King

Queen

Princess

cradle

fairy

cottage

spindle

hedge

Use the pictures to tell the story in your own words, and then draw your own pictures.

Rapunzel

A Prince was riding his horse in the forest. He could hear someone singing. The voice was beautiful but the song was very sad. Where was the voice coming from? The Prince could not see anyone.

The Prince rode on. When he came to the middle of the forest, he could see a very tall tower. The voice was coming from a small window at the top. The Prince walked round and round the tower looking for a way in. There was no way in. The tower had no door.

The Prince went back to the forest the next day. He climbed a tree near the tower. He sat and listened to the voice which sang so sweetly and yet so sadly.

"If only I could see into the tower," said the Prince. "If only I could see who the voice belongs to."

Presently an old witch came out of the forest. The Prince stayed hidden and watched her.

She went to the foot of the tower. "Rapunzel!" she called. "Let down your hair!"

A long braid of golden hair came tumbling from the window at the top of the tower. It was so long it reached the ground.

The witch climbed the braid of golden hair as if it were a rope. When she reached the top she climbed into a room in the tower. She pulled in the braid of hair after her. "So that is the way into the tower," said the Prince.

Presently the braid of hair fell from the window again. The witch climbed down by it and went off into the forest. Someone inside the tower pulled the hair back again.

As soon as the witch had gone, the Prince went to the foot of the tower. "Rapunzel!" he called. "Let down your hair!"

The braid of hair came tumbling down, just as it had when the witch called. But this time it was the Prince who climbed it like a rope.

"I wonder who I will find at the top?" said the Prince to himself.

At the top of the tower was a tiny room. In the room was a beautiful girl. The long golden hair was hers. The witch had kept her in the tower since she was a small girl. She was a prisoner. That is why she sang so sadly.

"Tomorrow I will bring a ladder made from silk and help you to escape," said the Prince.

The old witch found out that Rapunzel had seen the Prince. She was very angry. She was very angry indeed. She wanted to keep Rapunzel hidden away from everyone.

"You will never see the Prince again!" she cried as she took a pair of scissors from the table.

She cut right through the braid of golden hair. It fell to the floor and lay in a shining heap. "Now let the Prince try to climb into the tower," cried the witch. Then because she was so angry, she banished Rapunzel to a far-away land.

Next day the Prince returned to the tower. "Rapunzel!" he called. "Let down your hair!" The long braid of golden hair came tumbling to the ground. The Prince thought Rapunzel had let it down.

The Prince began the long climb upwards. He had a silken ladder tucked inside his coat. Rapunzel would soon be free.

He had almost reached the window when he looked up, and saw the witch looking down at him. She was holding the braid of golden hair in her hands.

"You will never see Rapunzel again!" said the wicked witch. She opened her fingers and let the braid of golden hair slip through them. It fell to the stony ground far, far below. The poor Prince fell to the stony ground with it.

The Prince lay on the ground for a long time. When, at last, he opened his eyes he could not see. He was blind.

He wandered far and wide, thinking only of Rapunzel. He was very sad for he could not think of a way to help her.

Then one day, when he was far from home, he heard someone singing. The song was both sweet and sad. It was a song he had heard before. He could not see, but the Prince knew he had found Rapunzel.

Rapunzel kissed his blind eyes and he could see again.

The Prince took Rapunzel home to his castle and they lived happily ever after.
The spell of the wicked witch was broken and she was never seen again.

All these appear in the pages of the story. Can you find them?

Use the pictures to tell the story in your own words, and then draw your own pictures.

The Frog Prince

A Princess was playing with her golden ball. She dropped it. It rolled across the grass towards the pond. She ran after it.

Before she could reach it, it fell into the pond with a gentle plop.

The Princess knelt beside the pond. She looked down into the clear water. Her golden ball was lying at the bottom of the pond like a golden sun. She tried to get it out. The pond was too deep. She could not reach it. The Princess began to cry.

"Why are you crying?" asked a voice. The Princess looked around. There was a frog sitting on a rock beside the pond.

"Did you speak?" she asked.

"I did," said the frog.

The Princess told him what had happened to her ball.

"I will fetch your ball for you if you promise me three things," said the frog. "You must let me sit on your chair. You must share your food with me. You must let me lie on your bed."

"Of course I will, I promise," said the Princess. "Now, please, will you get my ball?"

The frog dived to the bottom of the pond.

He brought the golden ball back to the Princess. It was not easy for him. The ball was as big as he was.

The Princess took the ball from the frog. She danced off across the garden. She had already forgotten her promise. She did not give the frog another thought.

Next morning, everyone in the palace was getting ready for breakfast. The Princess was skipping along the corridor when she met the frog. "What are YOU doing in the palace?" she cried.

"You must now keep your promise," said the frog.

"Go back to the garden where you belong," cried the Princess. "I do not like you!"

She ran and hid behind the King. "Please make the frog go away," she said.

But when the King heard that the Princess had made a promise, he said, "A promise is a promise, and it must be kept. A promise to a frog is just as important as a promise to a king."

The King and his three daughters sat down to eat breakfast. The frog hopped to the side of the Princess's chair. "May I sit beside you?" he croaked. The King heard the frog speak and he looked sternly at the Princess.

The Princess picked up the frog.
"Do not drop me," he said.
"Do not drop him," said the King.

The Princess put the frog on the chair beside her, then moved as far away from him as she could.

"May I share your food?" asked the frog. The Princess put the frog on the table beside her own plate.

The frog ate a very good breakfast. The Princess ate hardly anything at all. Somehow, she did not feel very hungry.

When he had finished eating, the frog said, “I am tired. May I lie on your bed?”

The Princess did not answer. The King looked at her sternly. “A promise is a promise,” he said.

The Princess picked up the frog. She held him away from her and carried him to her bedroom.

The Princess could not bear to think of the frog sitting on her bed. She put him on a little chair away from her bed. She closed the bedroom door so that nobody could see what she had done.

"I will tell the King you have not kept your promise," croaked the frog. The Princess burst into tears. She could not help it. "I have let you sit on my chair, I have shared my food with you," she cried, "must I really let you lie on my bed?"

"A promise is a promise, as you very well know," croaked the frog. The Princess lifted the frog from the chair and threw him across the room.

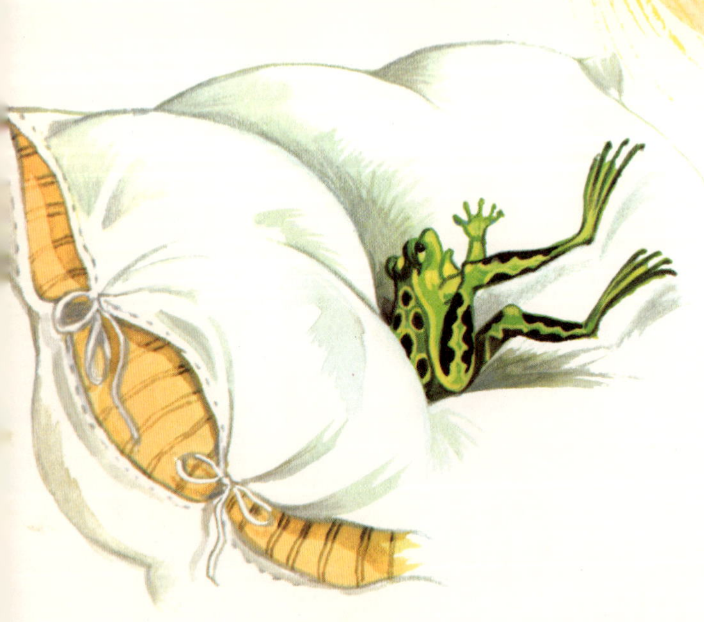

He fell onto her crisp white pillow. The Princess buried her face in her hands and cried.

She did not see the frog change into a Prince.

The Prince wiped away her tears. “By keeping your promise you have broken a spell cast by a wicked witch,” he said. “Now we can both live happily ever after.” And they did.

All these appear in the pages of the story. Can you find them?

Use the pictures to tell the story in your own words, and then draw your own pictures.

24

The Elves and the Shoemaker

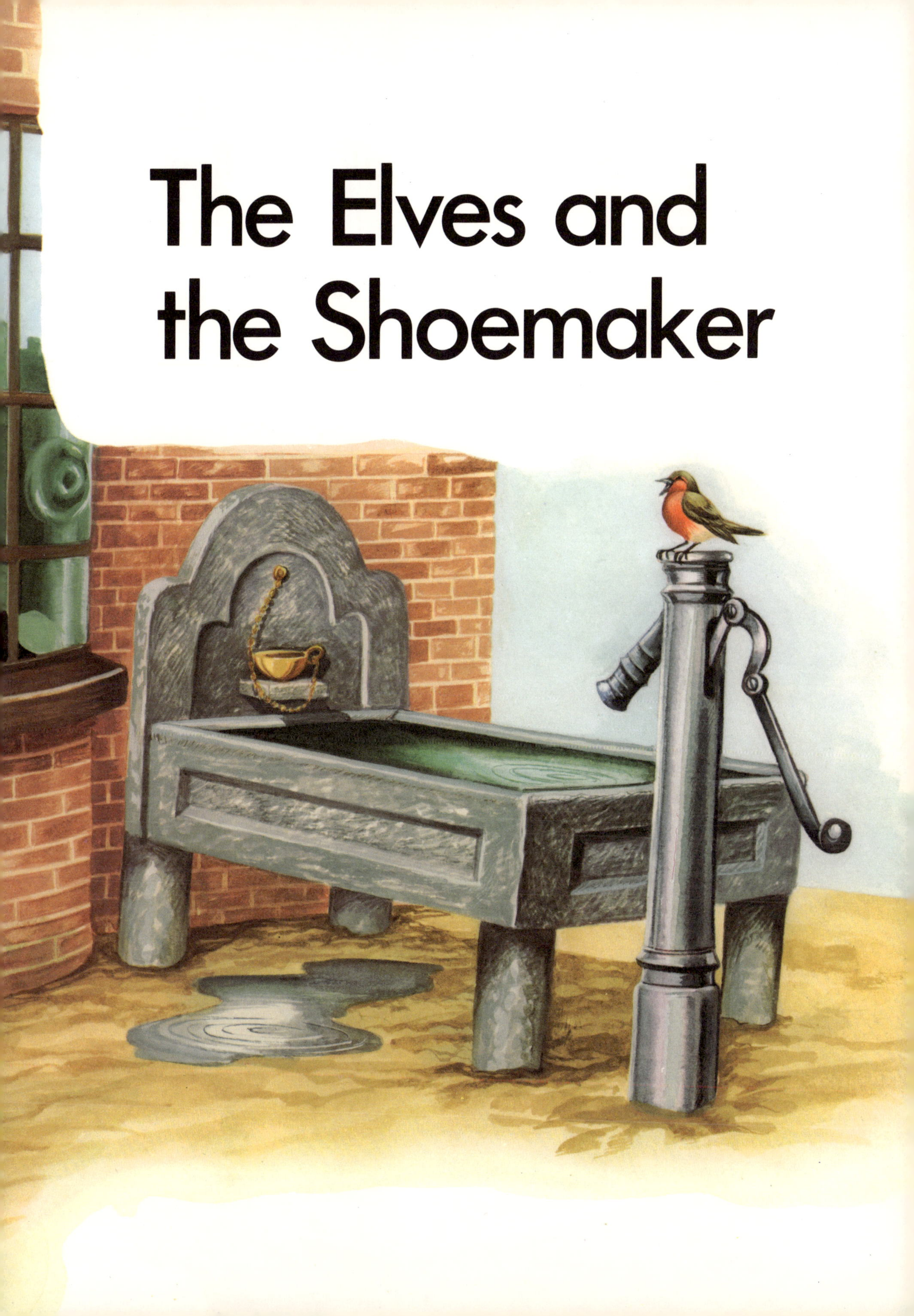

Once there was a shoemaker. He sat at his bench making shoes all day long. He worked very hard but nobody would pay him a fair price for the shoes he made. He and his wife were very poor.

One day, the shoemaker showed his wife a piece of leather.
"This is the last piece of leather I have," he said.
"When it is gone I will be unable to make any more shoes. We will get very hungry. We may even starve."
"No wonder you look so sad," said his wife. She was sad herself.

The shoemaker cut out the pieces for the last pair of shoes. He put them on the bench.

"It is late," he said. "Let us go to bed. I will sew the pieces together in the morning."

"Wife! Wife!" he called loudly next morning. "Come quickly!"

"What is it?" cried his wife.

She ran into the workshop. There on the bench was a beautiful pair of finished shoes.

"Did you get up in the night and make them?" she asked.

The shoemaker shook his head.

"Then how did they get there?" she asked.

"I do not know," said the shoemaker.

"Whoever made the shoes meant us to have them," said the shoemaker. "They would not have left them behind otherwise."

He took the shoes to market. He sold them for a very good price. He and his wife would not starve that day, or the next.

When the shoemaker had bought food, he had enough money left to buy leather for TWO more pairs of shoes.

He cut the pieces for the new shoes and laid them on the bench. "I will sew them tomorrow," he said.

"Wife! Wife! Come quickly!" called the shoemaker next morning. "It has happened again!"

"I don't believe it!" said the shoemaker's wife. There, on the bench, were two pairs of finished shoes.

"Look how well they are made," said the shoemaker. "There isn't a stitch out of place."

"Fine shoes for sale!" he cried when he got to the market place. "Fine shoes for sale!"

He sold both pairs in the first five minutes he was there. He was paid a very good price for them too. That day he bought enough leather to make four more pairs of shoes.

And so it went on. Every night the shoemaker left pieces of leather on the bench. Every morning they had been sewn into shoes. Every day he bought more leather.

One day, the shoemaker's wife said, "I do wish we knew who is making the shoes for us. We owe everything to them. I would like to say thank you."

"I know how we can find out," said the shoemaker.

That night he put the pieces of leather on the bench as before. He put out the light, as before. But instead of going to bed, as before, the shoemaker and his wife hid in the darkest corner of the room and waited. At midnight two little elves stepped in through the open window.

They sat cross-legged on the bench and began to sew. They did not waste a minute. When they had put the last stitch into the last shoe they slipped away as quietly as they had come.

The shoemaker and his wife hurried to the window.

"We must find a way of thanking them," said the shoemaker.

"The poor little things," said his wife. "Did you notice how ragged their clothes were? And did you notice they had no shoes?"

"I will make them shoes," said the shoemaker.

"And I will make them each a set of clothes," said his wife.

The shoemaker took the finest, softest piece of leather he had, and made two pairs of tiny shoes. He had never made anything so small before.

The shoemaker's wife took the finest cloth she could find and made two sets of tiny clothes. She knitted two pairs of tiny stockings. She made two tiny hats. She had never made anything quite so small before.

By Christmas Eve everything was ready. That night the shoemaker put all the shoe leather underneath the bench. On top of the bench he put the two pairs of tiny shoes. His wife laid the two sets of tiny clothes beside them. Then they hid and waited for the elves to come.

When the elves saw what was on the bench they cried out in delight. "These must be for us!" they said. They took off their rags and dressed themselves in their new clothes. They put on their new shoes. They put on their new hats. And all the time they smiled and smiled.

The two happy little elves danced a merry jig all along the bench.
"Now we are no longer poor,
Cobbling we will do no more,"
they sang.
Then they skipped out through the window and were gone.

The shoemaker and his wife never saw the elves again. But their luck had changed. The shoes the shoemaker made, sold as well as the shoes the elves had made. They were never poor again and lived happily ever after.

All these appear in the pages of the story. Can you find them?

shoemaker

shoemaker's wife

shoes

bench

leather

elves

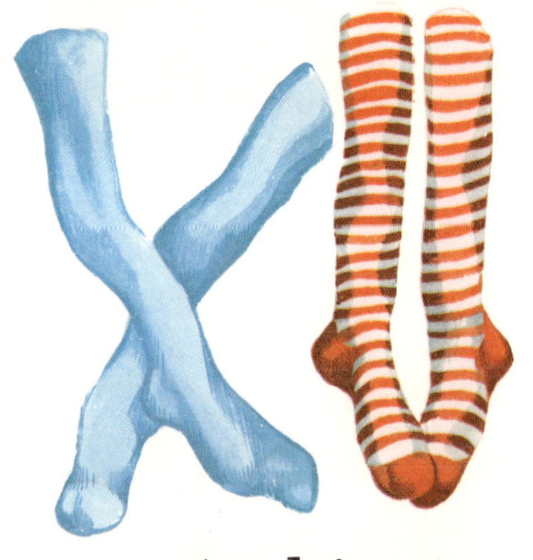

stockings

hats

Use the pictures to tell the story in your own words, and then draw your own pictures.